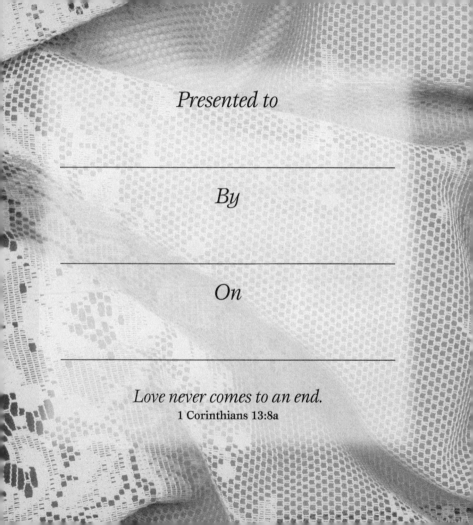

Presented to

_____

By

_____

On

_____

Love never comes to an end.
1 Corinthians 13:8a

The Book on Love

Developed and produced by The Livingstone Corporation. Project staff include: Christine Collier Erickson, Betsy Rossen Elliot, and C. Hudson. Cover design by JMK Associates. Interior design by Design Corps.

ISBN 0529-107260

Library of Congress Catalog Card Number 96-61531

Published by: World Publishing, Inc.
              Grand Rapids, Michigan 49418 U.S.A.
              All rights reserved.

Printed in the United States of America

1 2 3 4 5 6 7 8 00 99 98 97 96

Table of Contents

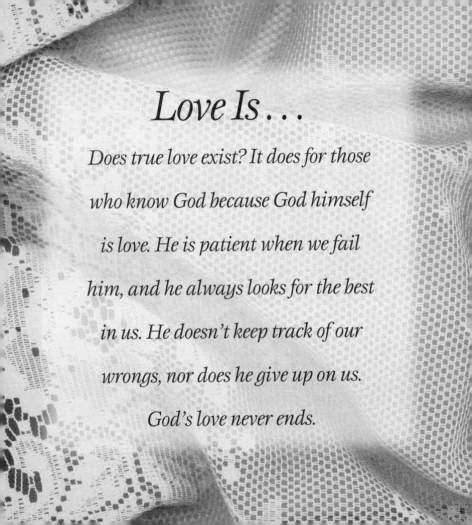

Love Is...

Does true love exist? It does for those who know God because God himself is love. He is patient when we fail him, and he always looks for the best in us. He doesn't keep track of our wrongs, nor does he give up on us. God's love never ends.

This is love: not that we have loved God, but that he loved us and sent his Son to be the payment for our sins.

1 John 4:10

We have known and believed that God loves us. God is love. Those who live in God's love live in God, and God lives in them.

1 John 4:16

No fear exists where his love is. Rather, perfect love gets rid of fear, because fear involves punishment. The person who lives in fear doesn't have perfect love.

1 John 4:18

Love is patient. Love is kind. Love isn't jealous. It doesn't sing its own praises. It isn't arrogant. It isn't rude. It doesn't think about itself. It isn't irritable. It doesn't keep track of wrongs. It isn't happy when injustice is done, but it is happy with the truth. Love never stops being patient, never stops believing, never stops hoping, never gives up.

Love never comes to an end.

1 Corinthians 13:4-8a

We understand what love is when we realize that Christ gave his life for us. That means we must give our lives for other believers.

1 John 3:16

The person who doesn't love doesn't know God, because God is love.

1 John 4:8

The greatest love you can show is to give your life
for your friends.

John 15:13

Love each other. This is what I'm commanding you
to do.

John 15:17

God's Gift of Love

God has given you the greatest gift

anyone could give! Out of his immense

love, God sent his Son to be the perfect

sacrifice for your sins. God's gift

enables you to spend eternity with him.

Why not accept his gift? It's the best

one you'll ever receive.

God loved the world this way: He gave his only Son
so that everyone who believes in him will not die
but will have eternal life.

John 3:16

Christ died for us while we were still sinners. This
demonstrates God's love for us.

Romans 5:8

Live in love as Christ also loved us.

Ephesians 5:2a

Consider this: The Father has given us his love. He
loves us so much that we are actually called God's
dear children. And that's what we are. For this
reason the world doesn't recognize us, and it didn't
recognize him either.

1 John 3:1

However, when God our Savior made his kindness and love for humanity appear, he saved us, but not because of anything we had done to gain his approval. Instead, because of his mercy he saved us through the washing in which the Holy Spirit gives us new birth and renewal.

Titus 3:4-5

God has shown us his love by sending his only Son into the world so that we could have life through him.

1 John 4:9

I have been crucified with Christ. I no longer live, but Christ lives in me. The life I now live I live by believing in God's Son, who loved me and took the punishment for my sins.

Galatians 2:19b-20

This is the reason I kneel in the presence of the
Father from whom all the family in heaven and on
earth receives its name. I'm asking God to give you a
gift from the wealth of his glory. I pray that he
would give you inner strength and power through
his Spirit. Then Christ will live in you through faith.
I also pray that love may be the ground into which
you sink your roots and on which you have your
foundation. This way, with all of God's people you
will be able to understand how wide, long, high, and
deep his love is. You will know Christ's love, which
goes far beyond any knowledge. I am praying this so
that you may be completely filled with God.

Ephesians 3:14-19

God Loves You

No matter whose love has fallen short of

your expectations, no matter who has

hurt you, you can know that a perfect

love does exist. Since before you were

born, your Father in heaven loved you.

He cares deeply for you, his child, and

has recorded that love in his word.

We love because God loved us first.

1 John 4:19

Even when you're old, I'll take care of you.
Even when your hair turns gray, I'll support you.
I made you and will continue to care for you.
I'll support you and save you.

Isaiah 46:4

Can a woman forget her nursing child?
Will she have no compassion on the child
     from her womb?
Although mothers may forget,
    I will not forget you.

Isaiah 49:15

The LORD appeared to me in a faraway place and said,

"I love you with an everlasting love.
So I will continue to show you my kindness."

Jeremiah 31:3

I love those who love me.
Those eagerly looking for me will find me.

Proverbs 8:17

The LORD . . . loves those who pursue righteousness.

Proverbs 15:9b

"I loved you," says the LORD.

Malachi 1:2a

The Father loves you because you have loved me and
have believed that I came from God.

John 16:27

Before the Passover festival, Jesus knew that the
time had come for him to leave this world and go
back to the Father. Jesus loved his own who were in
the world, and he loved them to the end.

John 13:1

The Blessings of God's Love

God wants to bless those who love him.

He is merciful, faithful, and compassionate.

Because you are a child of God, your

ultimate blessing is to have a position in

heaven with him. How wonderful to spend

eternity with your heavenly Father!

We know that all things work together for the good
of those who love God—those whom he has called
according to his plan.

Romans 8:28

I am convinced that nothing can ever separate us
from God's love which Christ Jesus our Lord shows
us. We can't be separated by death or life, by angels
or rulers, by anything in the present or anything in
the future, by forces or powers in the world above or
in the world below, or by anything else in creation.

Romans 8:38-39

The LORD, the LORD, a compassionate and merciful
God, patient, always faithful and ready to forgive.
He continues to show his love to thousands of
generations, forgiving wrongdoing, disobedience,
and sin.

Exodus 34:6b-7a

God our Father loved us and by his kindness gave us
everlasting encouragement and good hope.

2 Thessalonians 2:16a

But God is rich in mercy because of his great love for us.

Ephesians 2:4

God has brought us back to life together with Christ Jesus and has given us a position in heaven with him. He did this through Christ Jesus out of his generosity to us in order to show his extremely rich kindness in the world to come.

Ephesians 2:6-7

May the Lord direct your lives as you show God's love and Christ's endurance.

2 Thessalonians 3:5

But as Scripture says:

"No eye has seen,
  no ear has heard,
    and no mind has imagined
      the things that God has prepared
        for those who love him."

1 Corinthians 2:9

Because you love me, I will rescue you.
  I will protect you because you know my name.
When you call to me, I will answer you.
  I will be with you when you are in trouble.
  I will save you and honor you.
  I will satisfy you with a long life.
  I will show you how I will save you.

Psalm 91:14-16

The LORD protects everyone who loves him,
    but he will destroy all wicked people.

Psalm 145:20

Love the LORD, all you godly ones!
    The LORD protects faithful people,
        but he pays back in full those
            who act arrogantly.

Psalm 31:23

Our Lord was very kind to me. Through his kindness he brought me to faith and gave me the love that Christ Jesus shows people.

1 Timothy 1:14

But from everlasting to everlasting,
the Lord's mercy is on those who fear him.
His righteousness belongs
to their children and grandchildren,
to those who are faithful to his promise,
to those who remember to follow his
guiding principles.

Psalm 103:17

The Lord will bless you and watch over you.
The Lord will smile on you and be kind to you.
The Lord will look on you with favor
and give you peace.

Numbers 6:24-26

May the LORD God of your ancestors make you a thousand times more numerous, and may he bless you as he has promised.

Deuteronomy 1:11

The LORD is good.
  ⌊He is⌋ a fortress in the day of trouble.
  He knows those who seek shelter in him.

Nahum 1:7

Loving God

Sometimes loving God is difficult. It's easy to let other people and things take your attention away from God. But above everything else, you are to love God with your entire being—mentally, emotionally, and spiritually. What will result from such love?

Obedience, loyalty, respect, and worship.

I love you, O Lord, my strength.

Psalm 18:1

As a deer longs for flowing streams,
   so my soul longs for you, O God.

Psalm 42:1

As long as I have you,
   I don't need anyone else in heaven or on earth.

Psalm 73:25

I love the Lord because he hears my voice,
   my pleas for mercy.

Psalm 116:1

Love the Lord your God with all your heart, with all
your soul, and with all your strength.

Deuteronomy 6:5

But if they love God, they are known by God.

1 Corinthians 8:3

Israel, what does the L ORD your God want you to do? He wants you to fear him, follow all his directions, love him, and worship him with all your heart and with all your soul.

Deuteronomy 10:12

Love the L ORD your God, obey him, and be loyal to him. This will be your way of life, and it will mean a long life for you in the land that the L ORD swore to give to your ancestors Abraham, Isaac, and Jacob.

Deuteronomy 30:20

"Teacher, which commandment is the greatest in Moses' Teachings?"

Jesus answered him, " 'Love the Lord your God with all your heart, with all your soul, and with all your mind.' This is the greatest and most important commandment."

Matthew 22:36-38

To love him with all your heart, with all your understanding, with all your strength, and to love your neighbor as you love yourself is more important than all the burnt offerings and sacrifices.

Mark 12:33

Promises to Those Who Love God

Even though promises are easy to make yet

not always kept, your heavenly Father is

faithful to keep all his promises. Read in

God's word the evidence that he honors every

promise. Praise God for the promised

crown of life that he has for you!

"The mountains may move, and the hills may shake,
but my kindness will never depart from you.
My promise of peace will never change,"
says the LORD, who has compassion on you.

Isaiah 54:10

Keep in mind that the LORD your God is ⌊the only⌋
God. He is a faithful God, who keeps his promise
and is merciful to thousands of generations of those
who love him and obey his commands.

Deuteronomy 7:9

If you listen to these rules and faithfully obey them,
the LORD your God will keep his promise to you and
be merciful to you, as he swore to your ancestors.
He will love you, bless you, and increase the number
of your descendants. He will bless you with children. He will bless your land with produce: grain,
new wine, and olive oil. He will bless your herds
with calves, and your flocks with lambs and kids.
This will all happen in the land the LORD will give
you, as he swore to your ancestors.

Deuteronomy 7:12-13

LORD God of heaven, great and awe-inspiring God,
you faithfully keep your promise and show mercy to
those who love you and obey your commandments.

Nehemiah 1:5

There is lasting peace for those
who love your teachings.
Nothing can make those people stumble.

Psalm 119:165

Blessed are those who endure when they are tested.
When they pass the test, they will receive the crown
of life that God has promised to those who love him.

James 12:12

Don't love money. Be happy with what you have
because God has said, "I will never abandon you or
leave you."

Hebrews 13:5

Loving Others

Love for others is not limited to a feeling; it

requires action. It's being the listening ear

when someone needs to talk or a praying

friend when tragedy strikes. Although

loving others can be difficult work, the first

step is choosing to treat others' needs as

being as important as your own.

Above all, be loving. This ties everything together perfectly.

Colossians 3:14

I'm giving you a new commandment: Love each other in the same way that I have loved you. Everyone will know that you are my disciples because of your love for each other.

John 13:34-35

Dear friends, we must love each other because love comes from God. Everyone who loves has been born from God and knows God.

1 John 4:7

Dear friends, if this is the way God loved us, we must also love each other. No one has ever seen God. If we love each other, God lives in us, and his love is perfected in us.

1 John 4:11-12

Love each other as I have loved you. This is what I'm commanding you to do.

John 15:12

Whoever says, "I love God," but hates another believer is a liar. People who don't love other believers, whom they have seen, can't love God, whom they have not seen. Christ has given us this commandment: The person who loves God must also love other believers.

1 John 4:20-21

This is his commandment: to believe in his Son, the one named Jesus Christ, and to love each other as he commanded us.

1 John 3:23

He answered, " 'Love the Lord your God with all your heart, with all your soul, with all your strength, and with all your mind. And love your neighbor as you love yourself.' "

Luke 10:27

Never get revenge. Never hold a grudge against any of your people. Instead, love your neighbor as you love yourself. I am the LORD.

Leviticus 19:18

Pay your debts as they come due. However, one debt you can never finish paying is the debt of love that you owe each other. The one who loves another person has fulfilled Moses' Teachings. The commandments, "Never commit adultery; never murder; never steal; never have wrong desires," and every other commandment are summed up in this statement: "Love your neighbor as you love yourself." Love never does anything that is harmful to a neighbor. Therefore, love fulfills Moses' Teachings.

Romans 13:8-10

Love each other with a warm love that comes from the heart. After all, you have purified yourselves by obeying the truth. As a result you have a sincere love for each other.

1 Peter 1:22

Honor everyone. Love your brothers and sisters in the faith. Fear God. Honor the emperor.

1 Peter 2:17

Finally, everyone must live in harmony, be sympathetic, love each other, have compassion, and be humble.

1 Peter 3:8

Above all, love each other warmly, because love covers many sins.

1 Peter 4:8

The message that you have heard from the beginning is to love each other.

1 John 3:11

Continue to love each other.

Hebrews 13:1

Loving Your Enemies

Not everyone is easy to love. It's easier to ignore or repay people who have harmed us than to love them. But God commanded us to love our enemies. He calls us to care for them and to refuse to hold a grudge. We are to actively love others, treating our enemies as we would a friend.

But I tell everyone who is listening: Love your enemies. Be kind to those who hate you.

Luke 6:27

Rather, love your enemies, help them, and lend to them without expecting to get anything back. Then you will have a great reward. You will be the children of the Most High God. After all, he is kind to unthankful and evil people.

Luke 6:35

You have heard that it was said, "Love your neighbor, and hate your enemy." But I tell you this: Love your enemies, and pray for those who persecute you. In this way you show that you are children of your Father in heaven. He makes his sun rise on people whether they are good or evil. He lets rain fall on them whether they are just or unjust. If you love those who love you, do you deserve a reward? Even the tax collectors do that!

Matthew 5:43-46

Hate starts quarrels,
    but love covers every wrong.

Proverbs 10:12

Whenever you see that the donkey of someone who hates you has collapsed under its load, don't leave it there. Be sure to help him with his animal.

Exodus 23:5

If your enemy is hungry, give him some food to eat, and if he is thirsty, give him some water to drink.

Proverbs 25:21

Make sure that no one ever pays back one wrong with another wrong. Instead, always try to do what is good for each other and everyone else.

1 Thessalonians 5:15

Loving Your Family

Every family has problems, but God wants

us to look beyond the faults of our family

members and to love them anyway.

This requires that nagging, put-downs,

disobedience, and yelling be replaced with

encouragement, praise, obedience,

and kindness.

Husbands, love your wives as Christ loved the church and gave his life for it.

Ephesians 5:25

So husbands must love their wives as they love their own bodies. A man who loves his wife loves himself.

Ephesians 5:28

But every husband must love his wife as he loves himself, and wives should respect their husbands.

Ephesians 5:33

Husbands, love your wives, and don't be harsh with them.

Colossians 3:19

Tell older women . . . to be examples of virtue. In this way they will teach young women to show love to their husbands and children.

Titus 2:3-4

Two people are better than one because ⌊together⌋ they have a good reward for their hard work. If one falls, the other can help his friend get up. But how tragic it is for the one who is ⌊all⌋ alone when he falls. There is no one to help him get up.

Ecclesiastes 4:9-10

That's why a man will leave his father and mother and be united with his wife, and the two will be one.

Ephesians 5:31

But Ruth answered, "Don't force me to leave you. Don't make me turn back from following you. Wherever you go, I will go, and wherever you stay, I will stay. Your people will be my people, and your God will be my God. Wherever you die, I will die, and I will be buried there with you. May the LORD strike me down if anything but death separates you and me!"

Ruth 1:16b-17

Children, obey your parents because you are Christians. This is the right thing to do. "Honor your father and mother."

Ephesians 6:1-2

Do everything with love.

1 Corinthians 16:14

Romantic Love

Flowers, affection, and terms of endearment—all these are expressions of romantic love. While this love is fresh and exciting, romance alone may not stand the test of time. But when love develops from a deep commitment, it becomes a flame that cannot be extinguished.

My beloved is mine, and I am his.

Song of Songs 2:16a

Look at you! You are beautiful, my true love.
Look at you! You are so beautiful.
    Your eyes behind your veil are like doves.
    Your hair is like a flock of goats
        moving down Mount Gilead.

Song of Songs 4:1

You are beautiful in every way, my true love.
    There is no blemish on you.

Song of Songs 4:7

My bride, my sister, you have charmed me.
You have charmed me
    with a single glance from your eyes,
    with a single strand of your necklace.
How beautiful are your expressions of love,
    my bride, my sister!
How much better are your expressions of love
    than wine
    and the fragrance of your perfume than any spice.

Song of Songs 4:9-10

Wear me as a signet ring on your heart,
    as a ring on your hand.
Love is as overpowering as death.
Devotion is as unyielding as the grave.
    Love's flames are flames of fire,
        flames that come from the L ORD.
            Raging water cannot extinguish love,
                and rivers will never wash it away.
If a man exchanged all his family's wealth for love,
    people would utterly despise him.

Song of Songs 8:6-7

My true love, I compare you to a mare among
    Pharaoh's stallions.
Your cheeks are lovely with ornaments,
    your neck with strings of pearls.

Song of Songs 1:9-10

Now, the king loved Esther more than all the other women and favored her over all the other virgins. So he put the royal crown on her head and made her queen instead of Vashti.

Esther 2:17

Whoever finds a wife finds something good
and has obtained favor from the LORD.

Proverbs 18:22

Enjoy life with your wife, whom you love.

Ecclesiastes 9:9a

Two people are better than one because ⌊together⌋ they have a good reward for their hard work. If one falls, the other can help his friend get up. But how tragic it is for the one who is ⌊all⌋ alone when he falls. There is no one to help him get up. Again, if two people lie down together, they can keep warm, but how can one person keep warm? Though one person may be overpowered by another, two people can resist one opponent.

Ecclesiastes 4:9-12a

Love and Obey

If you love someone, you probably desire to
please that person. In the same way, your
love for God will be evident as you honor
him. As your relationship with the Father
deepens, you will learn to obey his
commands, and your life will
testify of your love.

If you love me, you will obey my commandments.

John 14:15

Whoever knows and obeys my commandments is
the person who loves me. Those who love me will
have my Father's love, and I, too, will love them and
show myself to them. . . .

   Those who love me will do what I say. My Father
will love them, and we will go to them and make our
home with them.

John 14:21, 23b

If you obey my commandments, you will live in my
love. I have obeyed my Father's commandments, and
in that way I live in his love.

John 15:10

Love means that we live by doing what he commands. We were commanded to live in love, and you have heard this from the beginning.

2 John 6

We know that we love God's children when we love God by obeying his commandments. To love God means that we obey his commandments. Obeying his commandments isn't difficult.

1 John 5:2-3

Jesus asked him again, a second time, Simon, son of John, do you love me?

Peter answered him, "Yes, Lord, you know that I love you."

Jesus told him, "Take care of my sheep."

John 21:16

Love the L$_{ORD}$ your God, and do what he wants you to do. Always obey his laws, rules, and commands.

Deuteronomy 11:1

Carefully follow the commands and teachings that the L$_{ORD}$'s servant Moses gave you. Love the L$_{ORD}$ your God, follow his directions, and keep his commands. Be loyal to him, and serve him with all your heart and soul.

Joshua 22:5

I have carried out your commandments.
I have obeyed your written instructions.
I have loved them very much.
I have followed your guiding principles
    and your written instructions,
      because my whole life is in front of you.

Psalm 119:166b-168

Encouraging Love

Have you ever noticed that love is contagious? People who love are an encouragement to others. When you notice people who have grown weary of loving others, look for ways to love them. Pray for them, and encourage them to share God's great love.

My goal in giving you this order is for love to flow
from a pure heart, from a clear conscience, and from
a sincere faith.

1 Timothy 1:5

Remain in God's love as you look for the mercy of
our Lord Jesus Christ to give you eternal life.

Jude 21

As holy people whom God has chosen and loved, be
sympathetic, kind, humble, gentle, and patient. Put
up with each other, and forgive each other if anyone
has a complaint. Forgive as the Lord forgave you.
Above all, be loving. This ties everything together
perfectly.

Colossians 3:12-14

We also pray that the Lord will greatly increase your love for each other and for everyone else, just as we love you.

1 Thessalonians 3:12

We must also consider how to encourage each other to show love and to do good things.

Hebrews 10:24

You have heard the desire of oppressed people,
    O LORD.
    You encourage them.
    You pay close attention to them

Psalm 10:17

Learn to do good.
Seek justice.
Arrest oppressors.
Defend orphans.
Plead the case of widows.

Isaiah 1:17

If your gift is serving, then devote yourself to
serving. If it is teaching, devote yourself to teaching.
If it is encouraging others, devote yourself to giving
encouragement. If it is sharing, be generous. If it is
leadership, lead enthusiastically. If it is helping
people in need, help them cheerfully.

Romans 12:7-8

Love Your Friends

One of the greatest examples of Christ's love is giving your life for others. This love can be demonstrated in many ways: lending money, baby-sitting, or sharing a meal. To give your life for your friends means being available to assist however and whenever needed—no matter how uncomfortable it feels.

Friends can destroy one another,
    but a loving friend can stick closer than family.

Proverbs 18:24

Do not abandon your friend or your father's friend.
Do not go to a relative's home
    when you are in trouble.
    A neighbor living nearby is better
        than a relative far away.

Proverbs 27:10

The greatest love you can show is to give your life
for your friends. You are my friends if you obey my
commandments.

John 15:13-14

Loving God's Commandments

In God's commandments you find boundaries and guidelines. His teaching provides wisdom and guidance. Loving God's commands will result in a life that honors God and is filled with peace. Fill your heart with them for they are worth far more than gold.

Oh, how I love your teachings!
They are in my thoughts all day long.

Psalm 119:97

I love your commandments more than gold,
    more than pure gold.

Psalm 119:127

Your promise has been thoroughly tested,
    and I love it.

Psalm 119:140

I hate lying; I am disgusted with it.
I love your teachings.
Seven times a day I praise you
    for your righteous regulations.
There is lasting peace for those
      who love your teachings.
    Nothing can make those people stumble.

Psalm 119:163-165

I have obeyed your written instructions.
I have loved them very much.

Psalm 119:167

Keep in mind that the Lord your God is ⌊the only⌋ God. He is a faithful God, who keeps his promise and is merciful to thousands of generations of those who love him and obey his commands.

Deuteronomy 7:9

This is what I'm commanding you today: Love the Lord your God, follow his directions, and obey his commands, laws, and rules. Then you will live, your population will increase, and the Lord your God will bless you in the land that you're about to enter and take possession of.

Deuteronomy 30:16

Whoever knows and obeys my commandments is the person who loves me. Those who love me will have my Father's love, and I, too, will love them and show myself to them.

John 14:21

Showing Love

Think back to the last time you were shown love. Was it an unexpected act of kindness, a helping hand, or a listening ear? No matter how large or small the act, it meant more than mere words. God's word teaches us that we are to show our love through sincere actions.

You were indeed called to be free, brothers and
sisters. Don't turn this freedom into an excuse for
your corrupt nature to express itself. Rather, serve
each other through love.

Galatians 5:13

Dear children, we must show love through actions
that are sincere, not through empty words.

1 John 3:18

You don't need anyone to write to you about the
way Christians should love each other. God has
taught you to love each other. In fact, you are showing love to all the Christians throughout the prov-
ince of Macedonia. We encourage you as believers to
excel in love even more.

1 Thessalonians 4:9-10

Love sincerely. Hate evil. Hold on to what is good. Be devoted to each other like a loving family. Excel in showing respect for each other.

Romans 12:9-10

But the man wanted to justify his question. So he asked Jesus, "Who is my neighbor?"

Jesus replied, "A man went from Jerusalem to Jericho. On the way robbers stripped him, beat him, and left him for dead.

"By chance, a priest was traveling along that road. When he saw the man, he went around him and continued on his way. Then a Levite came to that place. When he saw the man, he, too, went around him and continued on his way.

"But a Samaritan, as he was traveling along, came across the man. When the Samaritan saw him, he felt sorry for the man, went to him, and cleaned and

bandaged his wounds. Then he put him on his own animal, brought him to an inn, and took care of him. The next day the Samaritan took out two silver coins and gave them to the innkeeper. He told the innkeeper, 'Take care of him. If you spend more than that, I'll pay you on my return trip.'

"Of these three men, who do you think was a neighbor to the man who was attacked by robbers?"

The expert said, "The one who was kind enough to help him."

Jesus told him, "Go and imitate his example!"

Luke 10:29-37

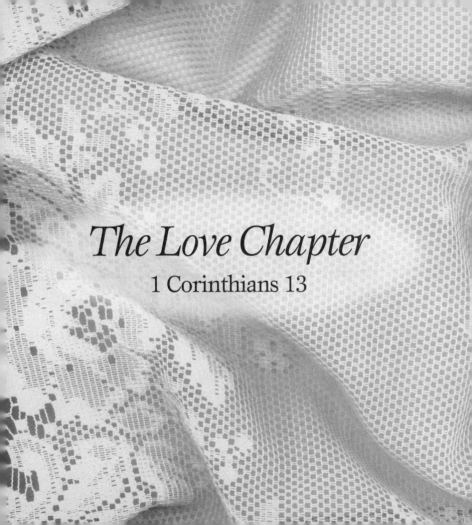

The Love Chapter
1 Corinthians 13

I may speak in the languages of humans and of angels. But if I don't have love, I am a loud gong or a clashing cymbal. I may have the gift to speak what God has revealed, and I may understand all mysteries and have all knowledge. I may even have enough faith to move mountains. But if I don't have love, I am nothing. I may even give away all that I have and give up my body to be burned. But if I don't have love, none of these things will help me.

Love is patient. Love is kind. Love isn't jealous. It doesn't sing its own praises. It isn't arrogant. It isn't rude. It doesn't think about itself. It isn't irritable. It doesn't keep track of wrongs. It isn't happy when injustice is done, but it is happy with the truth. Love never stops being patient, never stops believing, never stops hoping, never gives up.

Love never comes to an end. There is the gift of speaking what God has revealed, but it will no

longer be used. There is the gift of speaking in other languages, but it will stop by itself. There is the gift of knowledge, but it will no longer be used. Our knowledge is incomplete and our ability to speak what God has revealed is incomplete. But when what is complete comes, then what is incomplete will no longer be used. When I was a child, I spoke like a child, thought like a child, and reasoned like a child. When I became an adult, I no longer used childish ways. Now we see a blurred image in a mirror. Then we will see very clearly. Now my knowledge is incomplete. Then I will have complete knowledge as God has complete knowledge of me.

So these three things remain: faith, hope, and love. But the best one of these is love.

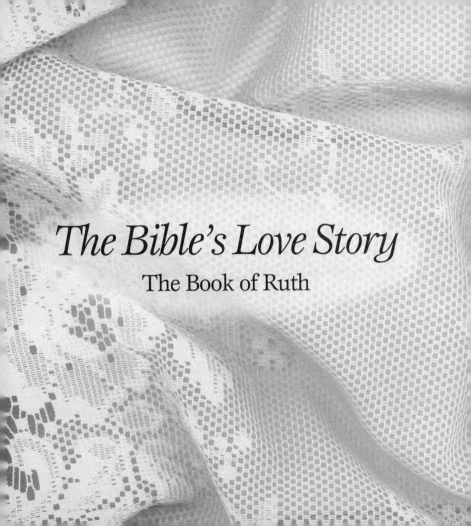

The Bible's Love Story
The Book of Ruth

Chapter 1

The Move to Moab and Tragedy

In the days when the judges were ruling, there was a famine in the land. A man from Bethlehem in Judah went with his wife and two sons to live for a while in the country of Moab. The man's name was Elimelech, his wife's name was Naomi, and the names of their two sons were Mahlon and Chilion. They were descendants of Ephrathah from Bethlehem in the territory of Judah. They went to the country of Moab and lived there.

Now, Naomi's husband Elimelech died, and she was left alone with her two sons. Each son married a woman from Moab. One son married a woman named Orpah, and the other son married a woman named Ruth. They lived there for about ten years. Then both Mahlon and Chilion died as well. So

Naomi was left alone, without her two sons or her husband.

Departure From Moab

Naomi and her daughters-in-law started on the way back from the country of Moab. (While they were still in Moab she heard that the LORD had come to help his people and give them food. So she left the place where she had been living, and her two daughters-in-law went with her.) They began to walk back along the road to the territory of Judah.

Naomi's Appeal to Her Daughters-in-law

Then Naomi said to her two daughters-in-law, "Go back! Each of you should go back to your mother's home. May the LORD be as kind to you as you were to me and to our loved ones who have died. May the LORD repay each of you so that you may find security in a home with a husband."

When she kissed them goodbye, they began to cry loudly. They said to her, "We are going back with you to your people."

But Naomi said, "Go back, my daughters. Why should you go with me? Do I have any more sons in my womb who could be your husbands? Go back, my daughters. Go, because I am too old to get married again. If I said that I still have hope. . . . And if I had a husband tonight. . . . And even if I gave birth to sons, would you wait until they grew up and stay single just for them? No, my daughters. My bitterness is much worse than yours because the LORD has sent me so much trouble."

They began to cry loudly again. Then Orpah kissed her mother-in-law goodbye, but Ruth held on to her tightly. Naomi said, "Look, your sister-in-law has gone back to her people and to her gods. Go back with your sister-in-law."

But Ruth answered, "Don't force me to leave you. Don't make me turn back from following you. Wherever you go, I will go, and wherever you stay, I will stay. Your people will be my people, and your God will be my God. Wherever you die, I will die, and I will be buried there with you. May the LORD strike me down if anything but death separates you and me!"

When Naomi saw that Ruth was determined to go with her, she ended the conversation.

Naomi Arrives in Bethlehem

So both of them went on until they came to Bethlehem. When they entered Bethlehem, the whole town was excited about them. "This can't be Naomi, can it?" the women asked.

She answered them, "Don't call me Naomi [Sweet]. Call me Mara [Bitter] because the Almighty has made my life very bitter. I went away full, but

the LORD has brought me back empty. Why do you call me Naomi when the LORD has tormented me and the Almighty has done evil to me?"

When Naomi came back from the country of Moab, Ruth, her Moabite daughter-in-law, came along with her. They happened to enter Bethlehem just when the barley harvest began.

Chapter 2

Ruth Gathers Grain in the Field of Boaz

Naomi had a relative. He was from Elimelech's side of the family. He was a man of outstanding character named Boaz.

Ruth, who was from Moab, said to Naomi, "Please let me go to the field of anyone who will be kind to me. There I will gather the grain left behind by the reapers."

Naomi told her, "Go, my daughter."

So Ruth went. She entered a field and gathered the grain left behind by the reapers. Now it happened that she ended up in the part of the field that belonged to Boaz, who was from Elimelech's family.

Just then, Boaz was coming from Bethlehem, and he said to his reapers, "May the LORD be with all of you!"

They answered him, "May the LORD bless you!"

Boaz asked the young man in charge of his reapers, "Who is this young woman?"

The young man answered, "She's a young Moabite woman who came back with Naomi from the country of Moab. She said, 'Please let me gather grain. I will only gather among the bundles behind the reapers.' So she came here and has been on her feet from daybreak until now. She just sat down this minute in the shelter."

Boaz Speaks With Ruth

Boaz said to Ruth, "Listen, my daughter. Don't go in any other field to gather grain, and don't even leave this one. Stay here with my young women. Watch where my men are reaping, and follow the young women in that field. I have ordered my young men not to touch you. When you're thirsty, go to the jars and drink some of the water that the young men have drawn."

Ruth immediately bowed down to the ground and said to him, "Why are you so helpful? Why are you paying attention to me? I'm only a foreigner."

Boaz answered her, "People have told me about everything you have done for your mother-in-law after your husband died. They told me how you left your father and mother and the country where you were born. They also told me how you came to people that you didn't know before. May the LORD reward you for what you have done! May you receive a rich reward from the LORD God of Israel, under whose protection you have come for shelter."

Ruth replied, "Sir, may your kindness to me continue. You have comforted me and reassured me, and I'm not even one of your own servants."

When it was time to eat, Boaz told her, "Come here. Have some bread, and dip it into the sour wine." So she sat beside the reapers, and he handed

her some roasted grain. She ate all she wanted and had some left over.

When she got up to gather grain, Boaz ordered his servants, "Let her gather grain even among the bundles. Don't give her any problems. Even pull some grain out of the bundles and leave it for her to gather. Don't give her a hard time about it."

Ruth and Naomi Talk About Boaz

So Ruth gathered grain in the field until evening. Then she separated the grain from its husks. She had about half a bushel of barley. She picked it up and went into the town, and her mother-in-law saw what she had gathered. Ruth also took out what she had left over from lunch and gave it to Naomi.

Her mother-in-law asked her, "Where did you gather grain today? Just where did you work? May the man who paid attention to you be blessed."

So Ruth told her mother-in-law about the person

with whom she worked. She said, "The man I
worked with today is named Boaz."

Naomi said to her daughter-in-law, "May the LORD
bless him. The LORD hasn't stopped being kind to
people—living or dead." Then Naomi told her,
"That man is a relative of ours. He is a close relative,
one of those responsible for taking care of us."

Ruth, who was from Moab, told her, "He also said
to me, 'Stay with my younger workers until they
have finished the harvest.' "

Naomi told her daughter-in-law Ruth, "It's a good
idea, my daughter, that you go out to the fields with
his young women. If you go to someone else's field,
you may be molested."

So Ruth stayed with the young women who were
working for Boaz. She gathered grain until both the
barley harvest and the wheat harvest ended. And
she continued to live with her mother-in-law.

Chapter 3

Naomi's Plan for Ruth's Marriage

Naomi, Ruth's mother-in-law, said to her, "My daughter, shouldn't I try to look for a home that would be good for you? Isn't Boaz, whose young women you've been working with, our relative? He will be separating the barley from its husks on the threshing floor tonight. Freshen up, put on some perfume, dress up, and go down to the threshing floor. Don't let him know that you're there until he's finished eating and drinking. When he lies down, notice the place where he is lying. Then uncover his feet, and lie down there. He will make it clear what you must do."

Ruth answered her, "I will do whatever you say."

Ruth at the Feet of Boaz

Ruth went to the threshing floor and did exactly as her mother-in-law had directed her. Boaz had eaten and drunk to his heart's content, so he went and lay at the edge of a pile of grain. Then she went over to him secretly, uncovered his feet, and lay down.

At midnight the man was shivering. When he turned over, he was surprised to see a woman lying at his feet. "Who are you?" he asked.

She answered, "I am Ruth. Spread the corner of your garment over me because you are a close relative who can take care of me."

Boaz replied, "May the LORD bless you, my daughter. This last kindness—that you didn't go after the younger men, whether rich or poor—is better than the first. Don't be afraid, my daughter. I will do whatever you say. The whole town knows that you are a woman who has strength of character. It is true

that I am a close relative of yours, but there is a relative closer than I. Stay here tonight. In the morning if he will agree to take care of you, that is good. He can take care of you. But if he does not wish to take care of you, then, I solemnly swear, as the LORD lives, I will take care of you myself. Lie down until morning."

Ruth Returns to Bethlehem

So Ruth lay at his feet until morning. Then she got up early before anyone could be recognized. At that moment Boaz thought to himself, "I hope that no one will ever know that this woman came to the threshing floor."

Then Boaz told Ruth, "Stretch out the cape you're wearing and hold it tight." So she held it tight while he measured out six measures of barley. Then he placed it on her ⌊back⌋ and went into the town.

When Ruth returned, her mother-in-law Naomi

asked, "How did things go, my daughter?"

Ruth told Naomi everything the man had done for her. She said, "He gave me these six measures of barley and told me not to come back to you empty-handed."

Naomi replied, "Stay here, my daughter, until you know how it turns out. The man won't rest unless he settles this matter today."

Chapter 4

Boaz Assumes Responsibility for Ruth

Boaz went to the city gate and sat there. Just then, the relative about whom he had spoken was passing by. Boaz said, "Please come over here and sit, my friend." So the man came over and sat down.

Then Boaz chose ten men who were leaders of that city and said, "Sit here." So they also sat down.

Boaz said to the man, "Naomi, who has come back from the country of Moab, is selling the field that belonged to our relative Elimelech. So I said that I would inform you. Buy it in the presence of these men sitting here and in the presence of the leaders of our people. If you wish to buy back the property, you can buy back the property. But if you do not wish to buy back the property, tell me. Then I will know that I am next in line because there is no

other relative except me."

The man said, "I'll buy back the property."

Boaz continued, "When you buy the field from Naomi, you will also assume responsibility for the Moabite Ruth, the dead man's widow. This keeps the inheritance in the dead man's name."

The man replied, "In that case I cannot assume responsibility for her. If I did, I would ruin my inheritance. Take all my rights to buy back the property for yourself, because I cannot assume that responsibility."

(This is the way it used to be in Israel concerning buying back property and exchanging goods: In order to make every matter legal, a man would take off his sandal and give it to the other man. This was the way a contract was publicly approved in Israel.) So when the man said to Boaz, "Buy it for yourself," he took off his sandal.

Then Boaz said to the leaders and to all the people, "Today you are witnesses that I have bought from Naomi all that belonged to Elimelech and all that belonged to Chilion and Mahlon. In addition, I have bought as my wife the Moabite Ruth, Mahlon's widow, to keep the inheritance in the dead man's name. In this way the dead man's name will not be cut off from his relatives or from the public records. Today you are witnesses."

All the people who were at the gate, including the leaders, said, "We are witnesses. May the LORD make this wife, who is coming into your home, like Rachel and Leah, both of whom built our family of Israel. So show your strength of character in Ephrathah and make a name for yourself in Bethlehem. Also, from the descendant whom the LORD will give you from this young woman, may your family become like the family of Perez, the son whom Tamar gave birth to for Judah."

Ruth Gives Birth to David's Ancestor

Then Boaz took Ruth home, and she became his wife. He slept with her, and the LORD gave her the ability to become pregnant. So she gave birth to a son.

The women said to Naomi, "Praise the LORD, who has remembered today to give you someone who will take care of you. The child's name will be famous in Israel. He will bring you a new life and support you in your old age. Your daughter-in-law who loves you is better to you than seven sons, because she has given birth."

Naomi took the child, held him on her lap, and became his guardian.

The women in the neighborhood said, "Naomi has a son." So they gave him the name Obed.

He became the father of Jesse, who was the father of David.

The Ancestry of David

This is the account of Perez and his family.

Perez was the father of Hezron.

Hezron was the father of Ram.

Ram was the father of Amminadab.

Amminadab was the father of Nahshon.

Nahshon was the father of Salmon.

Salmon was the father of Boaz.

Boaz was the father of Obed.

Obed was the father of Jesse.

Jesse was the father of **David**.

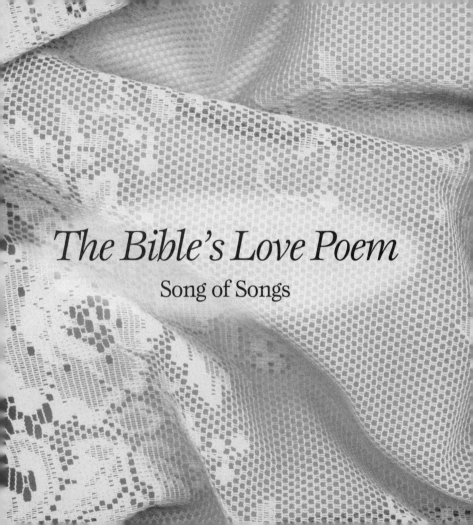

The Bible's Love Poem

Song of Songs

The most beautiful song of Solomon.

The Young Woman Arrives in Solomon's Palace

[Bride]

>Let him kiss me with the kisses of his mouth.
>>Your expressions of love are better than wine,
>>>better than the fragrance of cologne.
>>>>(Cologne should be named after you.)
>>No wonder the young women love you!
>>Take me with you. Let's run away.
>The king has brought me into his private rooms.

[The chorus of young women]

>We will celebrate and rejoice with you.
>We will praise your expressions of love
>>more than wine.
>How right it is that the young women love you!

[Bride]

Young women of Jerusalem, I am dark and lovely
like Kedar's tents,
like Solomon's curtains.
Stop staring at me because I am so dark.
The sun has tanned me.
My brothers were angry with me.
They made me the caretaker of the vineyards.
I have not even taken care of my own vineyard.
Please tell me, you whom I love,
where do you graze your flock?
Where does your flock lie down at noon?
⌊Tell me,⌋ or I will be considered a prostitute
⌊wandering⌋ among the flocks of your companions.

[The chorus of young women]

If you do not know, most beautiful of women,
follow the tracks of the flocks,

and graze your young goats near
the shepherds' tents.

Solomon Searches for the Young Woman's Love

[Groom]

My true love, I compare you to a mare
among Pharaoh's stallions.
Your cheeks are lovely with ornaments,
your neck with strings of pearls.

[The chorus of young women]

We will make gold ornaments with silver beads
for you.

[Bride]

While the king is at his table,
my perfume fills the air with its fragrance.
My beloved is a pouch of myrrh
that lies at night between my breasts.

My beloved is a bouquet of henna flowers
    in the vineyards of En Gedi.

[Groom]
    Look at you! You are beautiful, my true love!
    Look at you! You are so beautiful!
        Your eyes are like doves!

[Bride]
    Look at you! You are handsome, my beloved,
        so pleasing to me!
    The leaf-scattered ground will be our couch.
    The cedars will be the walls of our house.
    The cypress trees will be our rafters.

I am a rose of Sharon,
    a lily ⌊growing⌋ in the valleys.

[Groom]

    Like a lily among thorns,

        so is my true love among the young women.

[Bride]

    Like an apple tree among the trees in the forest,

        so is my beloved among the young men.

        I want to sit in his shadow.

            His fruit tastes sweet to me.

He leads me into a banquet room

    and looks at me with love.

        Strengthen me with raisins

            and refresh me with apples

                because I am weak from love.

His left hand is under my head.

His right hand caresses me.

Young women of Jerusalem, swear to me

    by the gazelles

or by the does in the field
>that you will not awaken love
>>or arouse love before its proper time.

The Young Woman Remembers One Spring Day With Her Beloved

[Bride]
>I hear my beloved's voice.
>>Look! Here he comes,
>>>sprinting over the mountains,
>>>racing over the hills.
>My beloved is like a gazelle or a young stag.
>>Look! There he stands behind our wall,
>>>peeking through the window,
>>>looking through the lattice.
>My beloved said to me,
>>"Get up, my true love, my beautiful one,
>>>and come with me.

Look! The winter is past.
The rain is over and gone.
Blossoms appear in the land.
The time of the songbird has arrived.
The cooing of the mourning dove is heard
        in our land.
The green figs ripen.
The grapevines bloom and give off a fragrance.
Get up, my true love, my beautiful one,
        and come with me.
My dove, in the hiding places
        of the rocky crevices,
        in the secret places of the cliffs,
let me see your figure and hear your voice.
Your voice is sweet,
        and your figure is lovely."

Catch the foxes for us,
    the little foxes that ruin vineyards.
        Our vineyards are blooming.

My beloved is mine, and I am his.
He is the one who grazes his flock among the lilies.
When the day brings a cooling breeze
    and the shadows flee,
    turn around, my beloved.
        Run like a gazelle or a young stag
            on the mountains that separate us!

The Young Woman Dreams About Searching for Her Beloved

[Bride]
    Night after night on my bed
        I looked for the one I love.
        I looked for him but did not find him.

I will get up now and roam around the city,
 in the streets, and in the squares.
I will look for the one I love.
I looked for him but did not find him.
The watchmen making their rounds
 in the city found me.
⌊I asked,⌋ "Have you seen the one I love?"
I had just left them when I found the one I love.
I held on to him and would not let him go
 until I had brought him
  into my mother's house,
  into the bedroom of the one
   who conceived me.

Young women of Jerusalem, swear to me
 by the gazelles
  or by the does in the field,
   that you will not awaken love
    or arouse love before its proper time.

A Description of the Royal Procession

[The chorus of young women]
    Who is this young woman coming up
        from the wilderness
    like clouds of smoke?
        She is perfumed with myrrh and incense
           made from the merchants'
           scented powders.
    Look! Solomon's sedan chair!
        Sixty soldiers from the army of Israel
           surround it.
    All of them are skilled in using swords,
        experienced in combat.
    Each one has his sword at his side
        and guards against the terrors of the night.
    King Solomon had a carriage made for himself
        from the wood of Lebanon.

He had its posts made out of silver,
    its top out of gold,
    its seat out of purple fabric.
Its inside—with inlaid scenes of love—
    was made by the young women
        of Jerusalem.
Young women of Zion, come out
    and look at King Solomon!
Look at his crown,
    the crown his mother placed on him
        on his wedding day,
    his day of joyful delight.

Solomon Is Charmed by the Young Woman

[Groom]

Look at you! You are beautiful, my true love.
Look at you! You are so beautiful.
    Your eyes behind your veil are like doves.

Your hair is like a flock of goats
    moving down Mount Gilead.
Your teeth are like a flock of sheep
    about to be sheared,
      sheep that come up from the washing.
        All of them bear twins, and not one
          has lost its young.
Your lips are like scarlet thread.
Your mouth is lovely.
Your temples behind your veil
    are like slices of pomegranate.
Your neck is like
    David's beautifully-designed tower.
    A thousand round shields belonging to soldiers
      are hung on it.
Your breasts are like two fawns,
    like twin gazelles grazing among the lilies.
When the day brings a cool breeze

and the shadows flee,
I will go to the mountain of myrrh
and the hill of incense.
You are beautiful in every way, my true love.
There is no blemish on you.
You will come with me from Lebanon,
from Lebanon as my bride.
You will travel with me
from the peak of Mount Amana,
from the mountain peaks in Senir
and Hermon,
from the lairs of lions,
from the mountains of leopards.
My bride, my sister, you have charmed me.
You have charmed me
with a single glance from your eyes,
with a single strand of your necklace.
How beautiful are your expressions of love,

my bride, my sister!
How much better are your expressions
    of love than wine
and the fragrance of your perfume
    than any spice.
Your lips drip honey, my bride.
    Honey and milk are under your tongue.
        The fragrance of your clothing is like
        the fragrance of Lebanon.
My bride, my sister is a garden that is locked,
    a garden that is locked,
    a spring that is sealed.
You are paradise that produces
    pomegranates and the best fruits,
    henna flowers and nard,
    nard and saffron,
    calamus, cinnamon, and all kinds of incense,
    myrrh, aloes, and all the best spices.

⌊You are⌋ a spring for gardens,
 a well of living water flowing from Lebanon.

[Bride]
 Awake, north wind!
 Come, south wind!
 Blow on my garden!
  Let its spices flow from it.
  Let my beloved come to his garden,
   and let him eat his own precious fruit.

[Groom]
 My bride, my sister, I will come to my garden.
 I will gather my myrrh with my spice.
 I will eat my honeycomb with my honey.
 I will drink my wine with my milk.
  Eat, my friends!
  Drink and become intoxicated
   with expressions of love!

The Young Woman Dreams of Marriage With Her Husband

[Bride]

> I sleep, but my mind is awake.
> Listen! My beloved is knocking.

[Groom]

> Open to me, my true love, my sister,
>> my dove, my perfect one.
> My head is wet with dew,
>> my hair with the dewdrops of night.

[Bride]

> I have taken off my clothes!
>> Why should I put them on ⌊again⌋?
> I have washed my feet!
>> Why should I get them dirty ⌊again⌋?
> My beloved put his hand through the keyhole.

My heart throbbed for him.
I got up to open for my beloved.
My hands dripped with myrrh,
and my fingers were drenched
with liquid myrrh,
on the handles of the lock.
I opened for my beloved,
but my beloved had turned away. He was gone!
I almost died when he left.
I looked for him, but I did not find him.
I called for him, but he did not answer me.
The watchmen making their rounds
in the city found me.
They struck me!
They wounded me!
Those watchmen on the walls took my
robe from me!

Young women of Jerusalem, swear to me
    that if you find my beloved
        you will tell him I am hopelessly lovesick.

[The chorus of young women]
    Most beautiful of women,
        what makes your beloved better
            than any other beloved?
    What makes your beloved better
        than any other beloved
            that you make us swear this way?

[Bride]
    My beloved is dazzling yet ruddy.
        He stands out among 10,000 men.
            His head is the finest gold.
            His hair is wavy, black as a raven.
            His eyes are set like doves bathing in milk.
            His cheeks are like a garden of spices,

a garden that produces scented herbs.
His lips are lilies that drip with myrrh.
His hands are disks of gold set with emerald.
His chest is a block of ivory covered
    with sapphires.
His legs are columns of marble set on bases
    of pure gold.
His form is like Lebanon, choice as the cedars.
His mouth is sweet in every way.
    Everything about him is desirable!
This is my beloved, and this is my friend,
    young women of Jerusalem.

[The chorus of young women]
Where did your beloved go, most beautiful
    of women?
Where did your beloved turn?
    We will look for him with you.

[Bride]

My beloved went to his garden,
to the beds of spices,
to graze his flock in the gardens
and gather lilies.
I am my beloved's, and my beloved is mine.
He is the one who grazes his flock among the lilies.

Solomon Desires the Young Woman More Than the Rest of His Wives

[Groom]

You are beautiful, my true love, like Tirzah,
lovely like Jerusalem,
awe-inspiring like those great cities.
Turn your eyes away from me. They enchant me!

Your hair is like a flock of goats moving down
from Gilead.
Your teeth are like a flock of sheep,

sheep that come up from the washing.
All of them bear twins, and not one
has lost its young.
Your temples behind your veil
are like slices of pomegranate.

There are 60 queens, 80 concubines,
and countless virgins,
but she is unique, my dove, my perfect one.
Her mother thinks she is unique.
She is pure to the one who gave birth to her.
Her sisters saw her and blessed her.
Queens and concubines saw her and praised her.

The Young Woman's Home in Shulam

[The chorus of young women]
Who is this young woman?
She looks like the dawn.

She is beautiful like the moon,
   pure like the sun,
      awe-inspiring like those heavenly bodies.

[Bride]
   I went to the walnut grove
      to look at the blossoms in the valley,
      to see if the grapevine had budded
         and if the pomegranates were in bloom.
   I did not know that I had become
      like the chariots of my noble people.

[The chorus of young women]
   Come back! Come back, young woman
      from Shulam!
   Come back! Come back so that we may look
      at you!

[Bride]

> Why do you look at me, the young woman
>> from Shulam,
>> as you look at the dance of Mahanaim?

[The chorus of young women]

> How beautiful are your feet in their sandals,
>> noble daughter!
> The curves of your thighs are like ornaments,
>> like the work of an artist's hands.
> Your navel is a round bowl.
>> May it always be filled with spiced wine.
> Your waist is a bundle of wheat enclosed in lilies.
> Your breasts are like two fawns,
>> twins of a gazelle.
> Your neck is like an ivory tower.
> Your eyes are like pools in Heshbon,
>> pools by the gate of Bath Rabbim.

Your nose is like a Lebanese tower
    facing Damascus.
You hold your head as high as Mount Carmel.
Your dangling curls are royal beauty.
Your flowing locks could hold a king captive.

Solomon Longs for the Young Woman's Affection

[Groom]
    How beautiful and charming you are, my love,
        with your elegance.
    Young woman,
        your figure is like a palm tree,
            and your breasts are like its clusters.
    I thought, "I will climb the palm tree
        and take hold of its fruit."
    May your breasts be like clusters on the vine.
        May the fragrance of your breath
            be like apples.

May your mouth taste like the best wine . . .

[Bride]

    . . . that goes down smoothly to my beloved
        and glides over the lips of those
           about to sleep.
I am my beloved's, and he longs for me.
Come, my beloved.
    Let's go into the field.
    Let's spend the night
        among the henna flowers.
    Let's go to the vineyards early.
    Let's see if the vines have budded,
        if the grape blossoms have opened,
        if the pomegranates are in bloom.
There I will give you my love.
The mandrakes give off a fragrance,
    and at our door are all kinds of precious fruits.

I have saved new and old things
   for you alone, my beloved.

If only you were my brother,
   one who nursed at my mother's breasts.
If I saw you on the street,
   I would kiss you, and no one
      would look down on me.
   I would lead you.
   I would bring you into my mother's house.
      (She is the one who was my teacher.)
   I would give you some spiced wine to drink,
      some juice squeezed from my pomegranates.
His left hand is under my head.
His right hand caresses me.

Young women of Jerusalem, swear to me
   that you will not awaken love

or arouse love before its proper time!

The Young Woman's Love for Her Beloved

[The chorus of young women]
Who is this young woman
    coming from the wilderness
with her arm around her beloved?

[Bride]
Under the apple tree I woke you up.
    There your mother went into labor with you.
    There she went into labor
        and gave birth to you!
Wear me as a signet ring on your heart,
    as a ring on your hand.
Love is as overpowering as death.
Devotion is as unyielding as the grave.
    Love's flames are flames of fire,

flames that come from the LORD.
     Raging water cannot extinguish love,
         and rivers will never wash it away.
If a man exchanged all his family's wealth for love,
     people would utterly despise him.

The Young Woman With Her Family and Her Beloved

[The brothers]
     We have a little sister, and she has no breasts.
     What will we do for our sister on the day
         she becomes engaged?
     If she is a wall, we will build a silver barrier
         around her.
     If she is a door, we will barricade her
         with cedar boards.

[Bride]

    I am a wall, and my breasts are like towers.
        So he considers me to be one
            who has found peace.
    Solomon had a vineyard at Baal Hamon.
    He entrusted that vineyard to caretakers.
        Each one was to bring 25 pounds of silver
            in exchange for its fruit.
    My own vineyard is in front of me.
        That 25 pounds is yours, Solomon,
            and 5 pounds go to those
                who take care of its fruit.

[Groom]

    Young woman living in the gardens,
        while your friends are listening to your voice,
            let me hear. . . .

[Bride]
Come away quickly, my beloved.
Run like a gazelle or a young stag
on the mountains of spices.